Interview Skills,
Quest
Résumé and CV Writing

HOW TO GET HIRED

The Step-by Step System: Standing Out from
the Crowd and Nailing the Job You Want

by

Richard Smith

www.ricksmithbooks.com

HOW TO GET HIRED

Table of Contents

Introduction

I am not a Recruitment Consultant or a Headhunter. I am an Employer, or at least I have been for most of my business life.

I have headed substantial global divisions in successful multinational companies, both Public and Private, and during my 35-year management career I have hired more than a thousand people in all kinds of businesses, in countries as diverse as Britain, America, Australia, South Africa, Spain, New Zealand, Poland, Switzerland, France, Taiwan, Indonesia, Singapore, China, Brazil, Mexico, and some you may never even have heard of. Admin Staff, Managers, Salespeople, Engineers, Software Programmers, Marketing People, Graphic Designers, Social Media Geeks, Secretaries And P.A.'s, Accountants, Lawyers, Chefs, Waiters, Cleaners, Receptionists, DJ's, Musicians, Bouncers, and even a few Go-Go Dancers.

Without exception, the candidates who got hired were the best fit for the job at the time, for three key reasons: The way that they presented themselves, from their letter of application, résumé, or CV; the manner in which they performed at interview; and the way in which they conducted themselves throughout the process.

In this book, I will teach you, from an executive perspective, how to make yourself irresistible to potential employers, what works and what doesn't, and how to set yourself apart from the pack. You'll learn why so many job applications never even reach the decision makers (and how to make sure that yours do) and why some people take months or years to find their dream job. It's a step-by step-system that will train you how to break through the barriers, score more interviews, and secure more high-quality job offers.

It's not a magic bullet, however by the time you've read and implemented these systems, you will be way ahead of everyone else who's out there competing with you. You'll know what the most important things are and you'll be doing them the right way. You'll understand what companies are really looking for when they start the recruitment process, and you'll know how to set yourself up to match and exceed their expectations.

So, what's the difference between this approach and the more readily available (and often very good) books you'll read by people from the Recruitment Business?

Simple really. Many Recruitment Consultants and Headhunters make their money based on volume. Only at the high-end of the industry are they really interested in you, the candidate, because those guys make their living from repeat business from the same few important clients, with whom their personal relationship is a huge factor in whether they're trusted to be retained on future assignments. They'll make tens (or in some cases hundreds) of thousands in commission, but only if the candidate stays in place for at least a year, which means they have to drill deep to ensure that they're not going to put the wrong candidate into a job which could have massive consequences for their client. In this case, you're a *product*, which the headhunter is essentially sourcing and re-selling to their client, who is the *customer*.

A large part the recruitment industry is simply a numbers game. Thousands of companies worldwide are constantly hiring people, and those that utilize outside firms to source their candidates are mainly interested in seeing as many people as possible who fit within the parameters of the job description. The recruitment agents cast huge nets in order to fill their candidate databases full of résumés, so they don't have to work so hard when a job becomes available.

Sophisticated software allows them to parse their files and spit out short-lists, which they then submit to the employer. Most of them don't coach candidates, or offer them very much by way of guidance, so all they are really doing (in the main) is to provide a conduit between companies and candidates, to save the companies time and energy in the initial search phase. That's why the term "body shop" is widely used in Employment Agency circles. It's a shop for bodies, hopefully warm ones!

That's not to understate their place in the food chain. Some corporations won't even entertain direct approaches from job-seekers, and recruit exclusively through retained agents and agencies, so you'll need to understand how to present yourself to an agency in order to get onto their database and show up in searches, when a job comes on the books which might be suited to your skill set. However, there are still plenty of companies that either recruit directly, or use a mixture of methods.

7

In the last decade, online services such as LinkedIn and Monster have completely revolutionized the way that recruitment and selection operates, and there's never been a better time to be in the jobs market. If you know how to use these websites properly, you can make massive advances in your job hunt, really fast. Finding vacancies, and being found by prospective employers, is much easier than it was when everything relied on middlemen. The techniques in this book will work fine in that online marketplace, although it's not specifically about that. However there are many other brilliant books that will teach you the technicalities of how to harness their powerful access to the millions of jobs that are now sourced exclusively online.

This book is about how to stand out and get yourself noticed in the recruitment and selection process, so that you'll tick more boxes for prospective employers, because that's how the vast majority of hiring gets done.

Because those hundreds of people that I hired over the years all managed to do that in one way or another.

That's how they got the job.

How Do They Do It?

We all know people that seem to be able to change jobs at the drop of a hat, and move effortlessly up the earnings ladder, but how do they do it?

These days, I talk to and counsel people of all ages, from all industries, about how to get a new job. Almost invariably, the reason they need to seek outside help is that it just isn't happening for them. And the main reasons? Either they aren't really trying; or they're trying but they're badly organized.

Younger people have a distinct advantage in the jobs market, and it's not because they're young! Anyone under thirty living in the developed world has never known the secure employment conditions that used to exist before the world changed with the Lehman Brothers crash, and the longest industrial slump in fifty years. In the same time-scale, the rise of online and the stratospheric demand for IT professionals has changed our notion of 'career' from something that our fathers and grandfathers regarded as the perfect lifestyle; choose a career, find a way in (either by qualification or trade skills) then stay there, probably with the same company, for decades, knowing that the pay off would be a comfortable retirement with an adequate pension.

The millennial experience is entirely different. Whereas twenty years ago a significant component of your employment desirability would be that you had at least three to five years in each of your previous jobs, that's all gone now in most industries. It's not at all unusual for people to move jobs every year, and staying somewhere for more than two years is the exception rather than the rule. Younger people have grown up in this environment, and it's completely natural to them. Similarly, many of them think nothing of moving from city to city, and even country to country to chase their career, and the net result of this mobility is their ability to climb the ladder much faster.

If you're older, there's something to be learned here. The agility of your typical twenty-something; street smart, tech savvy, but above all *mobile*, is their generation's greatest asset. Amongst all this mobility, these young, flexible workers also understand how to use the tools at their disposal. They network like never before, using social media in the main, and they focus on their early-years career development like guerillas, putting aside notions of location and loyalty in favor of tactics such as personal branding and a consummate drive to get ahead of the curve before they get sucked back into the mêlée of also-rans; flipping burgers or parking cars. They live a life without limits, and they want it all.

So the first message that you should take from this preamble is that if you are to successfully advance yourself, or alternately escape from your current unsatisfactory work situation, you need to treat it as a *mission*, and make it your number one priority, every day of your life until you achieve your objective. Unless you're the seventh son of a seventh son, it isn't coming to you automatically. You need to put on your armor, grab your sword, and get out there among the dragons.

Planning To Succeed

Even though I spent decades writing, pitching and presenting business plans and corporate strategies, I was never really much for setting my own personal objectives. Sure, I knew I wanted to live in a gorgeous penthouse apartment (I do) with a beautiful wife (tick) and drive an amazing car (I have two) but I never wrote down my goals, and as a consequence they probably took me longer to achieve. I was always too busy in the here-and-now to think about the route to my desires.

But as I got a little older and more in-control, and started to observe how really successful people achieved what they achieved, one common thread appeared everywhere. Successful, accomplished people will always tell you that the singular most important thing they did (and still do) is to write down their goals, objectives, and ambitions, and never to lose sight of what they were and are aiming for.

Guess what? It works.

I think the reason why people are resistive to this approach is because it's become a cliché, and even a mantra for the New Age movement, and that puts the more pragmatic amongst us off. But understand this; affirmation, religion, and spirituality are just tags that people apply to their belief system when they don't have any other way to explain the things that happen to them. And that's fine if it helps.

But even die-hard atheists understand that there's a vast

amount of psychology going on inside all of us, which can't be scientifically or rationally described. Whether you think it's God, Buddha, Allah, the Universe, or just your own internal biochemistry at work, the simple truth is that if you want to work towards a target, you first need to set the target, and the to remind yourself *in continuum* what the target is, otherwise you risk being distracted by all the other stuff that's going on around you. You'll lose sight of where you're trying to get to. It's called 'Taking Your Eye Off The Prize'.

You can choose to ignore this at your peril. It doesn't matter why it works, or how it works, or even if you believe it works; successful people swear by it and you should be modeling yourself on them. So just grab a pen, or open up Evernote, and let's get started.

You want a new job. That's fine. But it's way too broad, and it doesn't give you any clue how to get started on finding one.

First, before we get to planning, let's establish *why* you want a new job. It could be for one of several reasons;

1. You want or need to earn more money. This will usually be either because you want nicer things, a better place to live, more success with the opposite sex (or the same sex for that matter) or to climb out of an inadequate lifestyle. Cool. You deserve it. Financial advancement is a basic human right.

2. You hate your current job. Maybe you've tried to like it, but it just won't work for you. It's holding you back, bringing you down, stifling your capabilities, or maybe it simply depresses you to have to show up each day and

do something that simply doesn't fulfill you.

3. You want or need to relocate. Maybe you just fancy a change of scenery, or you want to be nearer the action, such as moving from the country to the city. Maybe you have a new relationship, or you want to get away from the hangover of an old one. Perhaps you want to build a brighter future for your kids. There are a million reasons to move, and if you don't embrace mobility, you may be limiting your options.

Whatever your motivation, this is (for most people) a major exercise, which might also involve some upheaval, and definitely a significant change of routine. So approaching it in a casual or haphazard way is probably not going to bring about the desired result. After all, you wouldn't 'wing it' if you were moving house or getting married. So why would you risk it with your career; every decision you make, especially in the early part of your work life, can and will have a far-reaching 'cause and effect' consequence down the road.

Think of it like this; nobody, ever, was born with the skills to drive a car or ride a motorbike. Sure, we might be able to work out the mechanics of which buttons to press and levers to pull to go forwards or backwards. But until we hit the road, with someone alongside us, we're idiots, relatively speaking. Similarly, not all of us are armed with the ingrained skills to navigate the world of work.

You need a plan.

Focus and Organization

In a moment we're going to get stuck into setting some practical goals and objectives, so that there's a target to aim for. Before we get to that, it's a good idea to make sure our tool-box is in good shape. Once you get going on your mission, there will be a lot of different things happening and most of them will be outside your direct control. You'll be partly pro-active, but mostly re-active, because the only things you will actually be able to control are the first few steps in the process.

Every book or web article about job-seeking encourages you to set up a tracking and organizational plan, so you keep track of your applications, correspondence, interviews, and so on. Most tell you to use a spreadsheet, such as Microsoft Excel, so you have a visual representation of the process. However, unless you're a whizz with Excel, you'll probably find it either too complex, or too limiting. Sure, you can list all the companies you apply to, the date of your application, and any significant events and actions along the way, but keeping it up to date will require you to sit down at your computer and physically update it as you go. It's not very portable, and it's not particularly friendly if you want to search for something important.

However, there is a software tool that will make your mission immeasurably easier to control, and help you keep track of everything in a much friendlier and more useable way. It's called Evernote, and it's free.

Evernote

For any kind of project requiring personal organization, I

recommend Evernote. This is a hugely capable digital version of your notebook, which enables you to gather information, web clippings, notes, photographs, audio clips, and almost anything that might be part of your project, into one extremely well-organized program which can synchronize across computers, tablets and smart phones.

Evernote can appear a little daunting at first and it requires a certain amount of commitment, not least of which is putting away your pen and paper notebook forever! But once you use it for a few days, you'll wonder how you ever lived without it. All the information you gather is available all the time.

When you're putting together your job plan, gathering research on prospective employers (more about that later), storing links to useful web pages (or even the pages themselves), and setting up tasks, checklists, pictures, infographics, different versions of your résumé or CV, and your own ideas, Evernote is there to swallow it all. The App puts everything into Notebooks, which you can organize, and allows you to quickly attach *tags* to everything, which gives you multiple ways to sort and search your material when you need it.

As with almost every software application I recommended, Evernote is available in a free version which is Ad-supported, however the paid Premium version is well worth the investment, because of the additional features and extra storage, and comes in at around $50 or £30 per year

If you really like carrying a notebook around with you, there's even a specific Moleskine Evernote notebook available, which cleverly integrates with the program, using your smart phone camera.

The massive advantage of Evernote is that, once you set it up, you have your information with you (via the cloud) wherever you are, on your PC, Mac, Laptop, Smartphone, or Tablet. Everything you enter or collect is synchronized across all your devices, which means you can always call up whatever you need in a couple of taps or keystrokes. It's always there.

Your Job Search Mission

S.M.A.R.T Goal Setting

SMART goal setting is a widely used system that works in almost any situation. It provides structure and ease of tracking to your mission, in this case your job search. Whereas if you don't commit your goals to some kind of system, it doesn't mean that you don't have them, but it prevents you from focusing on the important parts of what you're trying to achieve. Things get forgotten. Every part of your goals or objective, from the small steps to the strategic objective, becomes a part of your *desired reality.* If you can see it, you can probably do it!

In terms of job searching, SMART goal setting is one of the most effective and yet least used device. Most people don't do this, so if you can discipline yourself to follow it, you'll not only provide yourself with a structure, but you'll be operating at a more organized level than most of your competitors; and remember, everyone else who's out there searching for a new job is your competition.

Once you've decided on the outline of your mission, which is simply to find and secure the job you want, it's time to set up your specific intermediary goals. With the SMART system, you can easily and quickly evaluate and modify your objectives, wherever you are in the process.

What does S.M.A.R.T. stand for?

SMART is simply an acronym for the five key parts of your objective. To make your goal S.M.A.R.T., you'll need to define the contents of each of the following criteria: Specific, Measurable, Attainable, Relevant and Timely.

Let's get started. Using Evernote (or any other note-taking place you prefer) set up a note called "Objectives". Make sure it's prominent, and easy to refer back to, because you're going to be using it a lot.

There are (of course) five sections, and you need to fill them like this;

Specific

What exactly do you want to achieve? The more specific your description, the better your chance of achieving it. For example, your over-arching objective might be *I want to be a millionaire*. That's not an objective; it's a wish! A SMART objective might be more like; *I intend to increase my salary by 30% every year for the next ten years, so that I will have a net worth of a million bucks at the end of it.*

So your first task is to set up the *Specifics* of your mission. Ask yourself the following questions, and write down the answers (the answers here are examples only):

- **Describe exactly what it is you want to achieve:**

  To secure a new job in my industry (or a different industry) that is financially and/or socially better than the one I currently have (if you have one).

- **Where do you want to work?**

  My target location is Southern California; either San Diego, Greater Los Angeles, or the San Francisco Bay Area.

- **How will I do this?**

I will achieve my objective by preparing myself correctly, using a professional résumé, actively researching and contacting companies that interest me in the area, and devoting three hours every day until I achieve my goal.

- **When will I do this?**

  I will begin on Monday (date) and I will complete my mission by January 1st 2016. (Note: always use absolute positive statements of certainty. Never use 'I hope to' or 'I will try to'. You allow yourself the latitude to slip or fail if you do, and that is not an option, once you kick off this process.)

- **With whom will I do this?**

  Here you should write down a list of the Companies and/or Industry sectors that you intend to attack. You need specific targets in your cross hairs. It doesn't mean that you can't follow other opportunities, and you can add new items to the list as you go. But you must have some clearly defined 'destinations' at the beginning, to get yourself moving on the process itself. For example, if you are in the technology industries you might write:

  - *Dell Computer Corporation*

  - *Lenovo*

  - *Apple*

  - *Hewlett Packard*

- **Your Conditions and Limitations**

  - *The starting salary will be not less than $45,000*

  - *I am willing to work 6 days a week, but I will not work on Sundays*

- *There will be comprehensive medical cover for myself and my family*

- *I will commute up to one hour in each direction*

- *My employment will be a permanent contract*

You see what we've done here? We set up our 'reasonable' expectations so that we can define and focus on opportunities that conform to the objective. That is not to say that you cannot modify your requirements or compromise later down the road, but from your starting position you should have a clear framework of what you are prepared to consider, and what is unacceptable to you in your current mindset. Along the way, there will be people or organizations that will attempt coerce you into lowering your standards or expectations, and these are decisions you can make at the time (when there's an offer on the table) but for your own objectives, you need a framework that you can mentally align to. You won't be telling anyone else what these conditions and limitations are, but you will have them as a constant benchmark, to remind you where you were when you started the process.

- **Why do I want to achieve this goal?**
  - *I will achieve my goal in order to reach my full potential as a professional and as an individual.*

  - *I will achieve my goal in order to provide a more satisfactory standard of living for my family and myself.*

  - *I will achieve my goal in order to be happier and motivated to go on and achieve even more in the future.*

Again, we are using 'certainty' in our statements here so we don't allow ourselves any wriggle-room to fall short or fail.

The reasons you state here will never change. These are your primary motivators for embarking on the mission in the first place, and no matter what else may change along the way, its important to be able to look back at any point and remember why you are doing this.

- **What (if any) are the possible alternative ways of reaching my goal?**

    Personally, I don't like this question, because it allows ambiguity into the process, and that can lead to compromise that may derail you. I recommend you avoid it.

Measurable

Measurable means that you identify exactly what it is you will experience when you reach your goal. It means breaking it down into measurable elements. You'll need concrete evidence. *Being happier* is not evidence; *Being free at the weekends and having sufficient disposable income to race cars at the track* is!

Defining the physical manifestations of your goal makes it clearer, and easier to reach.

Attainable

Is your goal attainable? Is it really acceptable to you? Consider the effort, time, expense your goal will require against the rewards, and any other obligations and priorities you have in life.

Done right, you can do something that seems impossible and make it happen, by planning smartly and going all out to achieve it!

Aim high. The only limitations are those you place on yourself.

Relevant

Is reaching your goal relevant to you? Do you actually want to be the boss, be famous, be busy? Do you have the personality for it, and the energy reserves to sustain it?

If you're short of skills can you get trained? If you're short of resources, can you get what you need?

Most importantly, underneath it all,, why do you want this. What's your end-game, in terms of how it will ultimately shape your life?

Timely

Time is money! Set up deadlines for yourself, more detailed than the initial Specifics. The deeper you micro-manage your timetable, the easier it will be to look to it for guidance and reminders about where you need to be at every stage.

You will undoubtedly need to move some of your milestones around at certain moments. The last thing you want is to heap added stress on yourself because your timetable turns out to be unrealistic because of external factors. But you cannot remove milestones, ever. And the end game remains the same, and fixed.

This is your plan. Even if it's not elegant, and even if you can't get all the pieces to fit on day one, it's a helluva lot better than the plan you had before, isn't it!

Researching Your Targets

It might seem obvious to you that you should find out as much as you can about a prospective employer, but you'd be amazed how many people just don't bother! Remember at the beginning we said that the one of your core strategies is to stand out and gain an edge over the competitive candidates; well here is one of those opportunities to differentiate yourself, because at least half of your competition won't have done this.

So even basic knowledge will help narrow the field.

Of the thousands of interviews I've conducted over the last three decades, this was always one of my primary criteria for whether I took a candidate seriously.

There are three main areas where research is important;

Do I really want to work for this company?

On the surface, you may be attracted to a Company for many reasons. If a particular organization has ticked the boxes when you were setting up your goals, you may have only used superficial evaluation to select them. You're going to be making some life-changing decisions based on these selections, so in the same way that you wouldn't move in with somebody until you knew a lot more about them than you learned on your first few dates, you need to dig a bit deeper before you commit yourself to investing time and energy in trying to get through the door.

Big companies spend millions on advertising and PR to make themselves look attractive and desirable to the outside world. But there's often a disconnect between their outward-facing public façade and what really goes on inside. I have had this happen to me (I won't name the corporation) and I can tell you that it's a frustrating and mind-numbing experience when you get hired, and later discover that it's really a shitty place to work.

A few years ago I was headhunted by a huge global corporation, as head of International Sales and Marketing. I went through several months of interviews, crossing the Atlantic multiple times, and 'meeting the bosses' before they finally made me an offer, which was financially irresistible, and I took the job.

One of my key assets was my long experience in their industry, and my vast contact base, which I had built up over more than a decade of actually doing business in a nice way with a lot of important people. At every stage, the people on the other side of the desk had nodded enthusiastically when we discussed the various organizations where I was known and respected, and I was given the clear and unequivocal impression that this was an asset that they were hungry to acquire.

But Oh Dear; when I eventually got inside and started to try to work my contacts, I learned the awful truth. This particular corporation was extraordinarily litigious, particularly in the areas of patents and copyrights, and had a vast legal department with what appeared to be it's own P&L in the balance sheet. They were engaged in litigation with a good proportion of the other major players in the industry, and that meant doors were closing on me as fast as they had previously opened.

24

Allied to that, because of this litigious style of business, many of the other companies that I tried to introduce as customers were scared stiff of committing to work with us, because they feared that they would end up in an expensive, unwinnable law suit somewhere down the line if things went wrong.

Thirdly, because of the ongoing litigation in some cases, our company was restricted from using technologies in our products which were subject to patent disputes, so we were having to make things in a much more complex and expensive way, which dramatically impacted our cost base, and with the inevitable knock-on to our prices. And finally, when we eventually did close some big deals, and got into the nitty-gritty of contract negotiations, the restrictions placed on my sales team by the company's legal policies meant that some of the deals never made it, because the customers simply got fed up with the complexity of negotiation and went off to do business with somebody else.

In this case, I had made a massive personal commitment, relocated away from home, and totally disrupted my family life to work for them. Sure, they were paying me a fat-cat salary, but the daily frustration of having half the world closed for business was immense. Not only that, but I had recruited a crack team from my previous companies, and now I had not only my own frustration to deal with, but the task of trying to motivate a team who were essentially stranded. We had a fantastic brand and huge financial muscle, but we were limited to trying to sell to about 30% of the available market.

I lasted three years, but in the end I was compelled to leave because I simply couldn't make things happen to the best of my capabilities. I moved on, but it still took me at least a year to repair my own reputation in the industry.

Now the lesson for me was that I should have asked around before I started talking to them. A simple Google search on the company name (let's call them Acme Widgets) such as *acme widgets litigation* will tell you a lot about the way a company conducts itself out in the world. In the case of this example, even today, more than eight years on, that search throws up ten pages of results about their lawsuits and litigation tactics.

Another Google Search that you should make at the beginning is *acme disgruntled employees.* This is especially important in the case of large corporations. Now, there will always be people who feel hard done by when they leave or get fired, and the internet provides them with a ready and open platform to vent their opinions, so you have to take what you read with a pinch of salt. But generally there's no smoke without fire, so make the search and see what you find. Be objective, and try to sort the genuine, thematic grievances from the straightforward bellyaching that happen everywhere. But if you spot patterns, particularly if you find multiple examples of employees suing their former employers or taking them to employment tribunals, dig a little deeper and decide whether this is commonplace or isolated. Because once you get stuck inside a corporation that doesn't treat its employees fairly, or is even exploitative, you'll be back to square one and you may be a long way from home.

These are relatively extreme examples, and of course they

are only one aspect of researching a target employer.

On the more positive side, you absolutely must arm yourself with knowledge about what the Company does, its products, its markets and it's standing in its industry. More about that shortly.

Finding Your Entry Point

Back in the day, when job advertisements were found in newspapers, the usual first step to kick off an application was to write a letter of application. These days, you're more likely to be applying via an internet job site or through an employment consultancy, assuming that the job is already defined and the company are hiring.

However, when you set out on your mission, especially of you are targeting specific employers in particular locations, it may be that you will be applying speculatively.

In this era of large-scale unemployment, especially in the white-collar sector, you'll regularly hear people say "I applied for over a hundred jobs and never got a response from any of them!" Why do we think that is?

If you have identified target employers that fit your SMART criteria, the quickest way to defeat yourself is to settle for the apparent situation that they're either not hiring at all (nothing on the website) or the jobs they *are* advertising don't match your qualifications or experience.

However, if you've done your research, and you know that a particular corporation definitely employs people who do what you do, there's absolutely nothing wrong with sending an unsolicited application, and in fact it can often give you a huge advantage;

Let's say you are a junior Accountant, and your experience is mainly in procurement and purchasing departments. You want to work for Acme Widgets because the company ticks all your boxes in terms of size, industry, and location. You've done your research and it looks like people are generally happy there. But they aren't listing any relevant vacancies on their website or on any of the job sites.

Know this: people leave. It's as certain as sunrise that in any sizeable department of any substantial company, there will always be at least one or two people who are in the process of leaving, getting promoted, or under-performing and about to get fired. There's a constant churn of staff in every industry, and you can harness this effect to position yourself to take advantage of opportunities that might arise suddenly, but will definitely arise regularly.

Maybe someone is under-performing, but management hasn't yet had the time or energy to go through the process of recruiting a replacement, so they allow the situation to run on. Big companies, especially at middle management level, are often grossly inefficient, so this stuff happens all the time.

Perhaps there's an expansion plan in the department, or maybe the company itself is experiencing growth and the priorities aren't yet focused on growing the staff to accommodate the extra load. It's going to happen, but the process proper hasn't yet kicked off.

Or maybe there's some kind of restriction on using external recruitment organizations (this is very common), and that company relies on their internal process to find candidates via LinkedIn, or some other kind of search methodology. So they hire, but they do it sporadically. Mark my words, in the corporations I've worked in, there were *always* gaps in our staffing that needed to be filled, if anyone could tear themselves away from the core business long enough to make a fist of the project. More often than not, candidates would appear via unsolicited applications, or recommendations from other members of staff, and would regularly be hired 'outside policy'.

So your strategy should be to submit first-class unsolicited applications to any company that interests you, particularly if you can't find anything suitable on the more conventional job or career search online.

We'll come on to Résumés and CV's in a later section (it's a big subject) but for now we're concerned about how to identify the right point of entry, who may not be the person responsible for the actual hiring, but instead will be the person who is living with the problem, usually a line manager or department head of some kind.

First you need to find out who they are, how to get in touch with them, and (very important) whether they are actually at work at the time when you make your approach; not on vacation or sick leave, for example.

There is a bunch of ways that you can do this, but the quickest and simplest is to call the company switchboard. Get the telephone number from the company's website, LinkedIn page, or anywhere else that you can find it. I'm sure you are smart enough to do that.

While you're on LinkedIn, search on the Company's name, and sift through the profiles until you find someone whose title indicates that they are the right person to approach.

This is often easier than you think. Just go to LinkedIn and do a People search using the company's name. Scroll through the people until you find someone who looks like the hiring manager. If you can't find one, try searching for an internal recruiter, the head of staff or, the head of Human Resources. Address your initial application to that person. They're used to it, and they'll have a system for processing it.

If you're calling, there are good times to call, and there are definitely times not to call. You will always get a better response if you call when the person who will be answering the phone isn't stressed, overloaded, or getting ready to leave for the day. My favorite time to cold-call businesses has always been mid-afternoon and never on a Friday.

It's a sweeping generalization, but most commercial companies are busier and more energized in the morning. After lunch, things usually slow down, especially in front-of-house. You need to wait until everyone is back from lunch and locked up in their office or in a meeting, and then you'll usually find that the receptionist of telephonist is less busy, even bored. If you call around 3.30 pm, their resistance levels are lower, and it's easier to start a pleasant conversation and get the information you need.

You probably won't need any special tricks to get the receptionist or telephonist to give you a name. If you want to know who's in charge of Accounts, just ask. If you want to then go a little bit further, ask if you can be put through to his/her assistant or secretary. But beware; the *last* thing you want to happen at this stage is to be put through to the Manager themself, so make it clear that you're only looking for information so that you can send them something interesting or useful.

If you should unfortunately end up talking to the *Target*, what are you going to say? You won't be prepared, and asking for a job probably isn't going to get you the result you want. The problem with unsolicited telephone calls (so-called cold-calling) is that you have a very restricted communication channel, and the minute you open your mouth, the person on the other end is already on the defensive, and it's very easy for them to say no. Your objective in this approach is to set up an opportunity to present the *very best version* of you that you can, and in this case, that's your beautiful Résumé, with a slick, interesting cover letter. I would even go so far as to say that if you are put through (and these things usually happen very fast before you have time to respond), you hang up the phone and reset to the beginning.

When it comes to your actual application, your first inclination will probably be to e-mail it. And for all those other people who have taken the initiative to find out the information like you, they will do the same. The problem is that the person you are approaching, like almost everyone in the business world, is inundated with e-mail, all day, every day. Conversely, conventional mail is almost a novelty these days, and if it's packaged up professionally (so that it looks important) it will definitely reach the Manager's PA or Assistant at the very least. After that, it's about what falls out of the envelope when it's opened.

And if you really want to give yourself the very best chance of reaching your target, use a 'signed-for' delivery service, such as DHL or UPS. Nobody can afford to ignore courier deliveries. It may cost you a little more, but your hit rate will be much higher. This kind of initiative is what will separate you from the crowd. Nobody else will be thinking this way. First impressions count for a great deal, and this is something that you can do very easily.

Perfect Application Letters

Your cover letter, or letter of application, will be the first thing that's read. If you don't get past this stage, you could have the best résumé in the world, but it could be headed, at best, into a pile of unread correspondence, and at worst, directly into the bin. You get one shot.

Before we get into the content aspects, here are some general rules, which you must follow.

1. Never hand-write your letter. You're trying out stand out from the crowd, sure, but hand-written letters in the business environment are incongruous, and whilst you may come across the odd old-school manager who appreciates the novelty value, most will just think its weird.

2. Use a Word-Processor on your computer, or have someone else do it for you. Use a standard font; Aerial, Calibri, or Helvetica for a modern look, Times, Cambria, Georgia, or Book Antiqua for a more traditional style, for example if you are applying for a position in the legal department, or if you know that the person you are writing to is over fifty (like me). The idea is to match the *context* in as many ways as possible, and fancy or unusual fonts will create the wrong impression.

3. Take care of the print quality. White or light-cream paper is acceptable (nothing else), and if you only have cheap laser print paper at home, take your letter to an instant print-shop and have them put it on something more substantial. Remember, this is the first thing that will come out of your envelope and it's all part of making a

good impression. But don't go over the top.

4. You should stick to a traditional business-like layout. Your name and address should be laid out on the top right of the page, right justified. On the top left you should start with the date, in the format: 30th January 2015. You should then insert one or two blank lines, and type in the recipient's details, in the following format:

> Mr. John Smith
> Director; Legal Services
> Acme Widget Corporation LLC
> 1283 West Parkway
> Southville
> 12156 Co.

5. Leave another two or three blank lines, and begin your letter with: Dear Mr. Smith

6. Leave one more blank line, and begin your letter. Don't be tempted to put a subject line in your letter. You will see these all the time in business correspondence, but you should avoid it because if you were to write something like "Job Application", you are giving the recipient a chance to decide that they're not interested at that point, and you're done for before you got started.

7. Now, you need a killer opening sentence; something that's going to hook them and make them want to read your whole letter (which should never be longer than one sheet). The key elements that make up a killer application letter are these:

   a. Why you are interested in their company

b. What you can bring, right from the start

c. How you can personally relate to their product or service.

8. **Why you are interested in their company**; this is where your research comes in. You need to create empathy from the get-go. You might say something like:

I've been reading a lot about Acme Widgets in the press (or online) lately. It sounds like your expansion into Asia is really taking off. I'm hoping your success means you're growing your workforce too, and that's why I'm writing.

With an opening like this, you'll have ticked the first box, which is to get *engagement*. You've made it easy for the recipient to read on to the next paragraph.

9. **What you can bring.** Now this works well if there's already a job description for you to base you application around, but in this case we're talking about an unsolicited approach, so you'll need to have worked out what goes on in the department you're approaching. Try something like this:

For the past three years, I've learned my trade in (e.g. Procurement Accounting) at XYZ Corp in Milwaukee. However, I've gone about as far as I can, so reluctantly I've decided it's time to move up to the next level. My background is in tight financial discipline against rigorous deadlines, and if that's a key attribute for your department/company, maybe there would be a good fit? I've listed my specific experience in the attached résumé, which I hope you'll be able to take a moment to read.

Here, you're telling them that you know you'd be right

for their company, but without over-blowing your trumpet. It's confident, but modest. You've answered one of the fundamental questions; why are you changing jobs? You've implied that you're a happy, loyal employee (*reluctantly it's time to move up to the next level*), which also implies a little ambition, and you've stated the obvious (*tight financial discipline, rigorous deadlines*); two obvious 'yes' answers for any manager. You've packed a lot of information into a very compact paragraph, and you haven't given them any opportunity to dislike you or reject you on the basis of the information you provided, so they should now sail through to the end of your letter.

10. How you can personally relate to their product or service; this is challenging, because you need to generate empathy without sounding cheesy or weird. You might say something like:

    When I was young, my Uncle always had your widgets in his toolbox, and we used to play with them in his garage. Who knew back then that one day I'd have a chance to work for the company that made them!

    People love a story. It wraps them into your world in a small way, and if it's a comfortable place, it reflects on you as a person they can relate to.

11. That's enough. A short letter that does the job well will ensure that they will then take a look at your résumé. If you've done your job right, they'll already be thinking that you're *a good fit* and your résumé will be there solely for them to align the details of your past experience with the overall impression that you've created in your cover

letter.

12. Sign off with *Yours sincerely* if you're in the UK, or just *Sincerely* in the US. You should only capitalize the first letter, as in the *Yours sincerely* example above. Don't mess with this. *Yours truly, Sincerely yours,* or *Yours faithfully* are inappropriate in this context, where you know the persons name you are writing to. If you've to use *'Dear Sir'*, you haven't done your research properly.

13. Hand-sign your letter. It doesn't matter if your signature is only vaguely legible, as long as it's neat and compact. You should already have put your name at the top right (in your home address block)

Your Résumé / CV

Irrespective of whether you're sending an unsolicited application or applying for a defined vacancy, your CV or Résumé is the most important factor in whether you'll make it to interview. I've seen thousands over the past three decades, and I can state with absolute certainty that a poor CV will normally be headed straight to the trash.

Before we dig into the two key factors; Design and Content, in detail, know this. The first page of your Résumé is a 'snapshot of you. First impressions count for everything. Done right, it's a powerful took that will encourage your prospective employer to read more. Done wrong, and you'll turn off the reader before they even get to the content, and your mission is curtailed.

Here are the basic rules;

1. Your résumé is a summary of the most important data about you. The objective is to secure an interview, nothing more, nothing less. Nobody ever got hired straight off their résumé, but millions of applications fail because the résumé wasn't right, even when (in some cases) the applicant was ideally suited for the job.

2. Less is more. The reader makes a snap judgment based on something like 15-30 seconds of their initial view. So you need to get down to business quickly, and give them

something to work with in the first half page, or they won't go any further. You must avoid verbose or flowery language in your résumé; that's not what people want to read.

3. You résumé needs to be 'web-friendly'. Although it will often be read by a human being, especially in the case of an unsolicited application, many larger companies use online search tools to 'grade' applicants in the first pass, so you need to understand how to use keywords and phrases to make sure that yours ticks the digital boxes in the early stage of the process. This is especially true if you are applying for a position with lots of competition.

4. Your résumé needs to be tailored so that it matches the position (or type of position) you are applying for. However, you also need to balance this, especially in the case of an unsolicited application, with the possibility that the vacancy they have, or have coming up, might not be totally aligned with your current job or previous experience. This is especially true in area like finance and administration, where your core skills may well be suitable for any number of roles, and you don't want to rule yourself out of the running because you are too specific about your experience.

5. De-personalize. This sounds counter-intuitive, since your résumé is all about you. What it really means is that you need to figure out what the reader will be scanning for, and leave out any superfluous information that might turn some people off. One of the biggest mistakes I've come across over the years is people including irrelevant information about their hobbies and outside interests.

You are trying to get hired for a job, not become someone's new best friend. If the company wants to know what you do in your spare time, they'll ask you at interview. Nobody ever got hired because they owned a pair of matching cocker spaniels, or had been skiing in five different countries. More about that shortly.

6. Keep it brief. If you're young, it's likely that you can summarize your entire career in a single page. Regarding jobs you've had, your prospective employer is really only interested in your experience as it relates to their requirements. Continuity is important though; you can't leave huge gaps in your time-line because of irrelevance, so you'll need to find a way to spin things so it doesn't look like you've been in jail for a few years (unless you have, of course, and then you have an entirely different set of challenges, which is outside the scope of this book). If you've had a thirty-year career, and maybe ten or more jobs, you need to work carefully to make sure that it looks like a smooth chronological progression. More than three pages for any résumé is too much. Two are ideal. As a reminder, you're trying to get an interview, and if you succeed, there will be plenty of time to talk through the milestones of your life at that stage.

7. Your chronology should always work backwards. This sounds obvious to most people, but it's amazing how many otherwise intelligent applicants get this wrong. The first thing that people want to read, after the preamble, is your most recent experience. It's unlikely that anyone will be particularly interested in any more than three of your previous jobs. They're not really

interested in your journey. You may sometimes hear people recommending the use of 'functional résumés'. This is where you focus on your achievements, qualifications and other data instead of chronology. You may indeed be tempted to use this format if you have serious gaps. Don't. It won't work, and you'll be found out anyway.

8. Specifics; especially in commercial roles, people are interested in the numbers. If you've been successful, you need to highlight the data that backs up your claims. There is nothing useful about ambiguity. Of course, you may be forced to fudge a few things to cover something that may have been less than stellar in your past. We will look at ways to do this legitimately in the next section.

9. Keep your education brief. Again, you're really only as good as the last thing you did. If you have a PhD, that trumps your secondary education, so you might mention your school, unless it's particularly embarrassing, but you would major on your university or college. In this case, if you include dates it will only be used to measure your age, so in most cases it's unnecessary.

10. Never include references on your résumé. If you make it to the short-list, that will be the time when references become important, and you can phone round and prime people then. For now, it's just inappropriate.

11. It needs to look nice and read well. Here comes the design section.

Perfect Résumé Design

The main elements of a well-designed résumé are used in order to do two things;

1. Make it easy to read, and for the prospective employer to find out what they need to know quickly and easily. Over-fussy layouts, colors, columns and fancy fonts are inappropriate. These will just become distractions from the purpose of the résumé.

2. Create an impression of competence. Always use white paper, and make sure it's reasonable quality, again because first impressions count for a lot. Don't bind your résumé, instead use a single small staple in the top left corner to hold the pages together. Of course if you are submitting online, although the design and layout rules remain the same, the paper and stapling are irrelevant.

For the purpose of this exercise we will assume that you will be creating your résumé on a computer, probably using one of the common Word Processing programs, such as Microsoft Word, Apple Pages, or Apache Open Office Writer. All of these programs include templates, and you may be tempted to use one. Beware. Taking Word as an example, the ONLY template you should ever consider is the one called 'Simple Résumé' (Classic Résumé on Pages). Everything else is padding put into the program by the software company to add value.

Do it like this.

Your Personal Contact Details

You must always put your personal details at the top. Use

this format:

- Your Name (in Boldface and/or Capitals)
- Your Residential Address (as brief as necessary). If you live (for example) near a big City, but your residential address doesn't normally include it, you need to add it in. For example, I live in a town called Brentford, which is in Greater London, but the postal address doesn't include London. So I always add it, because people need to know quickly where you are located, and "Brentford, Middlesex, TW8" means nothing to a recruiter in (say) Switzerland.
- Your Postal Address or Box No. (if it's different)
- Your direct telephone number (usually your cell)
- Your e-mail address.

So, it should look something like this:

RICHARD SMITH
43 Tavistock Lane
Brentford
London
TW8 12AB
United Kingdom
+44 7856 546785
rick@ricksmithbooks.com

That's all you need. Don't put Skype names, Twitter handles, or anything else. It's unprofessional, and if these are appropriate at a later date, you can exchange them directly at that time.

Summary or Objective?

This is optional, but if you do it right, it's powerful. Since you understand how important it is to grab the attention of the recruiter right from the start, this will give them a strong flavor for who you are, what you're 'selling' and/or what it is you're seeking to achieve. Whatever you choose, you should use 'passive voice'. In other words, don't write "*I am* this, or *I've done* that." Write from an objective position. Here are some examples;

OBJECTIVE:

To secure a challenging and fulfilling supervisory or junior-management position with a respected corporation in the Precision Widgets industry, with accountability and responsibility that will encourage and facilitate further career development. (Here you should add headline qualifications;) Qualified to NVQ Level 5 in Production Line Management.

This is highlighting

1. Your commitment the prospective employer's industry where you are experienced.

2. Clearly illustrating that you understand that accountability and responsibility are key criteria.

3. Illustrating that you're ambitious, and committed to a long-term future with the company.

4. That you are qualified to do a job of this kind. This is your 'headline' qualification only, to get you past the first stage. The rest comes later.

Alternately…

SUMMARY:

An accomplished middle-management team leader with over ten years experience in delivering complex and challenging projects against rigorous deadlines. Focused on nurturing, retaining, and developing team members for positive collaboration and optimum performance. (Here you should add headline qualifications;) *Certified CPA and currently studying part-time for BSc in Applied Accountancy Practice.*

This is highlighting

1. Your understanding that performance and leadership are two of the main criteria that are sought and valued.

2. Demonstrating that you are team-oriented, and that your leadership is collaborative and social. It implies that you will be a nice person to work for/with, and that you're committed to the success and stability of the people around you.

3. That you are qualified to do a job of this kind, and that you are sufficiently ambitious and committed to further development of your own career. This is also about engendering respect for you.

These are only examples. Of course you will need to build your own version, based on the job, employer, industry, and your own assets. But the key objectives of this section are:

a. Keep it brief (no more than five lines) but pack in a lot. Don't waste words; when you have written the first draft, spend some time polishing it and compacting it, so you include as many action words and phrases as you can. Give it to your smartest friend to ensure sure it makes sense.

b. Make sure you accentuate the key element of your history or aspiration. If you have verifiable hard data of your success, for example: *'Led 60% increase in revenue achievement in my previous two roles'* or *'Winner of Widget Salesman of the Year awards in 2012 and 2014',* include it. People love numbers. But don't exaggerate or fabricate. Make sure that your references will confirm your figures if asked. And keep it brief.

c. If you are applying for a specified position, make sure your Introduction uses words and phrases that align with the stated requirements. Read the job description like a question, and write your response like answers. That is what the recruiter is looking for.

Imagine this as the first paragraph of an article that has caught your eye. You would make a judgment whether to invest time in reading the rest of the piece, or that it isn't what you're looking for, and turn the page.

Most important; you are a *stranger* to the reader. They won't be looking for nuance, and they may not understand context, especially if you're coming from a different industry, so be clear and complete in what you write. This is your own personal 'elevator pitch'.

Professional Experience

Next you will be listing your jobs, or how you spent the previous years if you weren't working. As we said at the beginning, this should be done in reverse chronological order. The heading for each item should include:

*   The Name of the Company and its location. If the company is not well known, or it's not obvious what they do, you may include a short (one line) additional description.

- The Year Dates you held the position

- The Job Title you held; this should be the title that can be confirmed by your references, and you may also include the Department or Division if you think it will help to place you in context for your prospective employer

It might look like this:

2004-2007 **XYZ WIDGET CORPORATION – Chicago**

Procurement Executive – Precision Engineering Division

If you have done several jobs in the same company, list them separately, especially if you had promotions and/or progressions.

Employment Details and Achievements

Because we are seeking the maximum impact and readership retention, again you need to be brief but incisive. You don't need to write a text description of the Company, your Department, or your specific roles. You've given a clear impression of yourself and your capabilities in your Introduction, and that's enough. If your reader has got this far, they're only interested in your achievements, and how what you have done in the past can add to their own business, or fill a gap in their personnel line up. So we go straight to bullet points, and use numbers and data to make our points, such as:

- *Managed procurement & purchasing team of fifteen, across three international sites.*

- *Accomplished 25% uplift in productivity, and 15% reduction in overall cost year on year.*

- *Led the implementation of company-wide F.I.F.O. (look it up) stock management, resulting in 45 day/$1.2m reduction in inventory in one year.*

Details like this are dynamite for a prospective employer. Everyone has something in their history that they can use here; you may have to think hard, but what did you do at your previous job that helped the company make or save money? That's what they're looking for, and many of the competitive candidates either won't have anything to say, or they won't even think to include the interesting stuff.

How Many Points and How Many Jobs?

If you are young, and you've only had one or two previous jobs, the idea is to fit your Résumé onto a single page, in 12pt text, with enough white space that it doesn't look cramped or cluttered. In your case, you should try to add as many bullet point achievements as it takes to make sure that the page looks complete (you'll need a little space at the bottom for any additional qualifications, memberships of professional bodies, and brief education details; three lines should be enough for most people (unless you're a scientist). But in no case should you use more than 5 bullets per position.

If you have more experience, perhaps four or five jobs over a ten-year period, you might use up to 5 bullets for the most recent and relevant job, but you should limit yourself to exactly 3 for each previous job. Remember, you're not trying to give them all the information they need to hire you, just enough to get your résumé to the short-list for interview, or to be passed from the Human Resources Department to the Functional Manger (your prospective new boss). So when you're composing your bullet points, write as many as you can think of, then go through and find the three that are a combination of the most impressive and the most relevant to the company or position you're applying for.

If you find you're running into more than two pages, you have an issue. I recommend that your detailed professional experience (the ones where you use bullet points) should only go back three jobs, or seven years, whichever is greater. Once you are back that far, you should still list the Dates, Companies, and Positions, but don't add any further detail. You may have turned the reader on with your recent experience, but you could just as easily turn them off if they have to churn through your early years. The numbers won't mean a lot, and there's an assumption that if you reached this level of qualification, experience and maturity, your early career is largely irrelevant.

What If You Have Gaps?

It's entirely possible you might have gaps in your professional or work chronology, for any number of reasons. The common ones are:

Unemployment

Back in the day, periods of unemployment were often viewed negatively by prospective employers, but with what has happened to the world over the last decade, recruiters are much more realistic about this now. However, you still need to handle this delicately on your résumé, especially if it runs into a few years.

If, for example, you were laid off by Ford in Detroit, and it took you two years before you were able to retrain, find a different job, or move cities, you can spin it positively. Every employer in the USA understands what happened in Detroit, so it's not what happened to you, it's what you did to correct it that will play positively for you. So, if there's a high-profile back-story, which puts your gap into context, mention it. If not, say nothing. If the rest of your résumé stands up, an employment gap a few years ago probably won't disbar you, though you'll need to be ready to describe and explain it at your interview, assuming you get one.

If your period of unemployment was less than six months and is bracketed by jobs, you don't need to put it on your résumé. But you will need to be prepared to disclose it at interview, if it comes up.

Illness, Family Responsibilities

If you were off work because of your own illness, or perhaps you took a career break to raise children, or to care for an ageing or sick relative, the simplest way to put this in your résumé is to write in your Professional Experience;

2001-2004 – Career Break; Family Responsibilities.

That's all you need. If you've made the shortlist, based on the other stuff, this won't affect that, especially if it's a few years ago. If they like you enough to care, you may be asked to expand on this, either in a pre-interview, or at the interview itself, and you'll need to have a strong explanation ready. That is covered in the section on Interview Questions. You can also use the term Sabbatical, if it's around one year. If you do, you'll need to be ready to explain, and it also helps to have something useful that you did during the time you weren't working. Again, if it's recent, you'll need detail on your résumé. If it's a few years ago, don't add any.

This can be tricky. Of course, all employers should absolutely respect anyone who has been in the service, irrespective of whether they have seen action or simply worked in the Pay Corps. The problem is that society is polarized, particularly since the Iraq wars, and where one prospective employer may be enthusiastic about your chest full of medals and the fact that you saved a hundred orphans from a burning village, another may be concerned that your latent PTSD is going to resurface in their business in the future. Human nature being what it is, my recommendation is that if you have military service in your history, unless it is directly and positively relevant to the position you are seeking, you play it down in your résumé to a one-liner, such as:

2001-2005 – United States Navy

This is the 'plain-vanilla' method that avoids judgment at this early stage. If you make it through this stage, which will probably have absolutely nothing to do with the fact that you were in the military, there will be plenty of opportunity to discuss this part of your career once you get in the interview room.

Now, I fully expect to have Reviewers tell me that I'm being irresponsible or disrespectful by recommending this way of handling it. Please; I'm not. If I had my way, every returning soldier, sailor or airman/woman would have an automatic job for life. Anyone who's put their life on the line to protect my personal freedoms deserves total respect and even positive discrimination in the workplace. But I'm a student of human nature, and I've witnessed these prejudices at first hand, so I'm simply suggesting a strategy that puts off any potential misjudgment until you are better positioned to give a full account of yourself, your skills, and your experience. You cannot assume that everyone will perceive your situation positively, so you need to be face to face with him or her so you can gauge the situation for yourself, and tailor your approach accordingly.

Of course, it's more likely that most people will be extremely interested in your military history, and keen to talk about how your experience contributes to your suitability for the role.

Incarceration

If you were in prison, you'll need to get help from the rehabilitation or probation service with this. I am simply not qualified to advise how to handle it. In most countries you are legally bound to disclose it, even though a spent conviction is normally protected by law from prejudicing your future employment.

Gap Summary

In summary, it's far from unusual to have gaps in your work history, especially these days. The key is to be able to explain them logically and without raising any read flags regarding your suitability for employment. Prospective employers are looking for reliability and consistency in candidates, and if you keep this in mind, you will be able to formulate the right way to deal with your own gaps, if you have them.

Always remember that just because you got away with it on your résumé, it doesn't mean it's gone away for good. You will inevitably be called upon to give a full explanation at some point in the process. You can accentuate positives, downplay negatives, and even spin it a little. But you cannot lie, because a professional recruiter or HR executive will know, and whilst they might not directly confront you, they may simply reject your application as not standing up to scrutiny.

Education and Qualifications

The final thing you need to put on your résumé is your Education and Qualifications.

Your main focus here should be on the *highest* education and qualifications you possess. So if you have a University education and one or two degrees (lucky, clever you) that is what you should focus on. Nobody will be interested in your High School.

If your apogee (look it up) is High School or College, that's what you put. Make sure you list qualifications that make sense in your country. Don't make stuff up, or inflate your grades, because once again that's technically illegal, and it'll definitely get you dropped off the shortlist (or even lose you the job you already scored) if it shows up in your references.

If you have a college or university degree *and* something like an MBA, you should be listing both. Dates are optional, and probably only relevant if you had either a gap in your education, or some other discontinuity.

It should look like this:

EDUCATION & QUALIFICATIONS

B.A. (2.1) Media and Production, Solent University, 2005

MBA International Business - Harvard Business School, 2010

or

International Baccalaureate – John Brown College, Minneapolis, 2007

or

Memberships etc.

If you are applying for your first job after school or college, you may need to bulk up your Education section with notable things that will be viewed favorably by a potential employer *if it's at least vaguely relevant* to the job you are applying for. Things like:

- Winner – Governors Science Prize 2007
- Chairman – School Debating Society 2010 & 2011

However, if you are already in employment, and if your school days are well behind you, don't put this stuff in. At the bottom of a list of professional experiences, it's inappropriate.

Being a member of the Freemasons, Rotary, Buffaloes, Manchester United Supporters Club, or anything similar, is a no-no on your résumé. Anything that gives people a chance to make a *social judgment* about you is dangerous, so don't be tempted.

Likewise, never put your IQ (if you know it) on a résumé. If it's high, they'll think you're a smart-ass, and if it's low, they'll think you're a dumb-ass. In any case, it's boastful, because unlike academic qualifications, it implies that you actively sought it out purely to be able to measure yourself against other people. That is to be avoided at all costs. In many corporations, you're going to be tested as part of the hiring process anyway.

One corporation I joined, I aced the parametric tests in the recruitment process. I knew I'd done well; everything just seemed to click that day. I was never told the actual results, and I'd always assumed it would be kept secret. But a few months later, the CEO let it slip in a management meeting that I had scored the highest ever in the company, and from that day forwards the attitude of some of my colleagues changed, mostly in a bad way.

If you are perceived as particularly clever in a professional situation (except perhaps in research science) it can invoke all kinds of strange jealousy and resentment, so let your actions do the talking, and keep your more sensitive issues under wraps. Just by the way, I have never thought of myself as any smarter than anyone else (there were some real rocket scientists in that company) and that was just a freak occurrence, but it didn't help when people found out about it.

So, now we've covered all the elements of your résumé. We've kept it simple, and relevant, which is what employers are looking for. Here are some final pieces of advice:

Using Keywords

We mentioned earlier that some large corporations, who might receive hundreds of applications for a position, use electronic scanning to filter résumés and applications. If this is the case, the filters are set up to look for relevant *keywords* and phrases, which match the requirements of the job or the specifics of the description.

If you have a job description, it's a good idea to sprinkle some relevant keywords in your application and résumé. You need to make sure that they read naturally and don't look obvious.

For example, if the job description says something like: '5 *years experience of procurement operations in a similar role'*, you should try to include the phrase '5 *years experience'* somewhere in your résumé and/or your application letter. If you can also squeeze in the words *'procurement operations'* and *'similar role'* somewhere else in your documents, that might help too.

Don't Include Your Picture

There's been an alarming trend, particularly in the USA, for adding your photograph to a résumé. Unless the job advertisement specifically asks for it, don't do it. It's another example where you set yourself up for judgment, and that lowers your chances of getting through the first stage of the process. You want people to focus on your qualifications, experience, and suitability for the role. If you show them a picture, human nature kicks in once again, and professionalism can go out of the window.

You might be thinking "I am very good looking!" and that might tempt you to use your picture as an asset. Please don't. It's a sad fact that human evolution hasn't actually progressed as far as we think it has, and our primeval DNA is still covertly programmed to judge our first visual impression of someone on their basis of suitability for mating, or alternately as competition for our place in the herd. I have actually come across corporate environments where managers will actively avoid hiring good-looking people of the opposite sex because they've experienced jealousy from their own spouse or partner in the past. One CEO I had openly told me to "hire the ugly ones" for my department, because in his view they were less likely to be disruptive or distracting to the young salesmen in the team!

Personally and professionally I found that then, and still find it now, and appalling and outdated state of affairs, but if you know it goes on, you really don't want to put yourself in the firing line. Whatever you like, your appearance becomes decreasingly important, the further you can move through the selection process.

So, you now have a complete Résumé (CV in the UK) which looks like this;

RICHARD SMITH
43 Tavistock Lane
Brentford
London
TW8 12AB
United Kingdom
+44 7856 546785
rick@ricksmithbooks.com

SUMMARY:

An accomplished middle-management team leader with over six years experience in delivering complex and challenging projects against rigorous deadlines. Focused on nurturing, retaining, and developing team members for positive collaboration and optimum performance. Certified CPA and currently studying part-time for BSc in Applied Accountancy Practice.

Professional Experience

2008-2014 **XYZ WIDGET CORPORATION – Chicago**
Procurement Manager – Precision Engineering Division

- Managed procurement & purchasing team of fifteen, across three international sites.

- Accomplished 25% uplift in productivity, and 15% reduction in overall cost year on year.

- Led the implementation of company-wide F.I.F.O. stock management, resulting in 45 day/$1.2m reduction in inventory in one year.

- **EDUCATION & QUALIFICATIONS**

- B.A. (2.1) Media and Production, Solent University, 2005

- MBA International Business - Harvard Business School, 2010

If you're sending your application out in paper form, print it and you're done. If, however, you're sending it in electronic form, you would be well advised to save it as a .pdf file. Never send the original Word file, unless the recruiter has specified this. Different computers and operating systems may display the same file in different ways, and all your attention to detail and formatting may be lost in the process, meaning your beautiful résumé looks completely different, and possibly unattractive at the other end.

This is one of the reasons why I have recommended that you keep your format simple, and text-only. The less fancy formatting you put in, the less chance of it being corrupted along the way. But if you are able to use a pdf file, you can guarantee that it will look exactly the same on every device, your formatting will be carried over uncorrupted, and no one can accidentally alter or delete any part of it. It is, essentially, *locked*.

Social Media – Opportunities and Threats

You may be well aware that many employers will check you out on Social Media, particularly LinkedIn, as a part of the early vetting process. If you have a picture on your LinkedIn profile (and you should), make sure it is modest and business-like. You don't want it to be a factor in the process, if you can avoid it.

Whilst we're on the subject of LinkedIn, and it is a big subject for another book entirely, you should make sure that your résumé matches your online profile as far as possible. Employers check it. And as far as other Social Media is concerned, particularly Facebook, if you are in your job-hunting mission, you must at the very least adjust your Privacy settings so that only your Friends can see your Newsfeeds and any personal stuff you might have posted.

Go through and clean out anything controversial, delete any embarrassing pictures of you falling drunk out of a taxi with your pants round your knees, and so on. We all know that nothing goes away forever, but just make sure that nothing compromising is visible to anyone looking for dirt on you. If you can live without it for a few weeks or months, it might be a good idea to suspend your Facebook account completely whilst you are in the process of finding your new job.

Religion & Other Prejudices

We live in secular, free countries, and everyone is entitled to their own beliefs about anything at all, particularly religion and faith. There's an interesting paradox when it comes to religion; those that have it are entirely comfortable with their faith and often see nothing wrong in displaying it openly on Social Media. They also have no issue with people that don't share their views, because most western religions are all about tolerance. That's cool.

But be aware that it doesn't necessarily work the other way around. In the workplace, you will definitely encounter people, some quite normal and upstanding, others quite bigoted and prejudiced, who don't have the same capacity for tolerance. Much as this might grind your gears, you need to understand that it exists, just as racism, sexism, ageism, and homophobia also exist. You're not on a crusade to eliminate these evils from society, you're on a mission to get hired, so you have to find a way to accommodate the attitudes of people who don't believe what you believe, and the easiest and most effective way to achieve this is don't put yourself out there in the first place.

A good example of this was Tony Blair, the former Prime Minister of Britain (one of the most popular and successful of all time, at the time; though history may not reflect his legacy quite the same way). So the story goes, around the time of the beginning of the Iraq war, Blair was being interviewed by a journalist who asked if his religious faith was a component of his bonding with George W Bush. As Blair, a committed and outspoken Christian, was beginning to answer, Alistair Campbell, his astute press secretary and a declared atheist, intervened with the statement, "We Don't Do God" which was to crop up more than once over subsequent years.

Blair saw no issue with invoking religion, even in a time of war. Campbell, on the other hand, tasked with steering his boss down the middle ground as the leader of a free and secular country, knew that religion would potentially be a polarizing issue with the public, and clamped down on it hard.

And so it is in society in general, and the workplace in particular. Irrespective of your own comfort with religion, others will not always see it that way, and may indeed view you as different to them. Rather than risk polarization that could see you bumped from a short list because of someone's inherent prejudices, it's better to remove it from the equation. So again, if your Facebook feed is full of Bible Quotes and Affirmations, hide them, or shut it down whilst you complete your mission.

As we said at the start; *Whatever it Takes.* If you can't live with this, you may need a different strategy.

LinkedIn

This is NOT a book about LinkedIn. There are plenty of other books on the subject, however it's important that you understand the basics of this revolutionary platform, since even if you are not using to find and apply for jobs, it will almost certainly be a factor in your mission at some point.

LinkedIn is the ultimate networking site for anything and everything to do with companies and jobs. If you don't already have LinkedIn account, go ahead to www.linkedin.com and open one. The basic account is free. There is also a premium option, which adds a number of features, most important of which it gives you the ability to send internal mails on the LinkedIn platform to other members. If you are on a serious job-seeking mission, you should definitely invest in LinkedIn Premium.

For job seekers who are really serious about using LinkedIn as the primary tool for moving to a new position, LinkedIn Premium for Jobseekers is a specific membership plan which you should take a look at. There is a monthly membership fee of approximately $50, but this gives you a range of powerful additional tools, which will really accelerate your project. You can usually get a one-month free trial of at least one of the premium packages.

As you develop your LinkedIn presence, you will increase the number of contacts in a similar way to how you would do it on Facebook. Of course, your contacts will have contacts of their own, and LinkedIn allows you to see these and access them via "in mail".

You will remember that in the first section we talked at length about how to identify the right person in an organization to send your application. Using LinkedIn correctly, you can often shortcut the manual process, and use the platform to identify your target using sophisticated search tools. I'm not sure that *everybody* in the business world is LinkedIn, however I have never failed to find the person I was looking for, and connect with them.

You can also search for jobs by company, region, and industry. Many corporations now *only* use LinkedIn to recruit, because the costs are significantly lower than using a search and selection firm or recruitment consultant.

You must also set up your own profile on LinkedIn, which can include pictures, your résumé, and all sorts of other information that will be useful once people start looking at you on the platform, which they inevitably will if you're applying for jobs. It's important that you spend some time making sure your profile is accessible and suitable, because if you're not there, you may not even make it on to some shortlists.

LinkedIn is important. It is also extremely easy to use, and the LinkedIn website has a whole library of instructional information, videos etc. Go over there now and take a look.

There are some excellent books on Amazon that will walk you step-by-step through the LinkedIn process and explain the best ways to use it.

Submitting and Following up Your Applications

So that's it. You've identified your target(s), written your killer Application Letter, added a beautiful Résumé, and sent it all off. Now you wait…

No you don't!

There's always a chance, as we said at the beginning, that your direct approach will land on your Target's desk on exactly the day that they've decided to set to work filling a position in their company or department. This does happen, but the odds are against it. Since you have specifically targeted a Company that's one that you'd like to work for, you now need to start hustling to make sure that you get noticed.

Here are two examples of how 'the hustle' works, and it's all the explanation you need to encourage you to keep active on your applications.

Quite early in my career, I was looking for a job as a mobile phone salesman in London. It was boom time in that industry, right at the start when the phones were new and very expensive, and there was a lot of money to be made in sales. I had previously applied to work for Vodafone, in response to an advertisement in the newspaper, and had gone through the application process, only to find, six weeks on, that I hadn't been selected (more fool you Vodafone. You missed your chance!).

When I received the rejection letter, I was devastated. Not only was it a job I really wanted, but also I was out of work, with no money coming in, and a mortgage to pay. I had sat on my hands waiting for them to invite me for interview, sure that I had the right qualifications and experience, but they had passed me over, for reasons best known to themselves.

But, I knew I wanted to work in that industry, so I looked around for other Companies in the same business, and found a smaller firm who looked like they were doing pretty well from the amount of advertising they were placing in the papers. I called their front desk, found out the name of the Sales Director, and sent off my CV and cover letter. After a week or so, nothing had happened, so I picked up the phone and called them.

I managed to get out through to the right guy, and asked him if he had my application. He said that he had a lot of applicants coming through all the time, but I was persistent and asked him that, since I lived nearby (I didn't, by the way), could I pop round for a quick chat the next day, to which he agreed if I didn't mind coming at seven in the evening, as he was so busy. Lesson one: if I hadn't called and hustled for the meeting, my unsolicited application might have never made it to the top of his pile.

I duly turned up to meet him, and we had a really great chat, which didn't really feel like an interview at the time. He told me that he'd be in touch in a few days. He gave me the impression that I'd done well, so I left there full of optimism.

The days went by, and turned into a week, then two weeks, and I could feel that old familiar feeling of disappointment coming back. In those days I was supremely confident in a face-to-face situation, but I was never very comfortable calling people on the phone. I always had this picture that they would resent the intrusion, and it held me back for years.

But by this stage I was frustrated, and starting to get a little desperate, so I plucked up the courage and made the call. I spoke to the receptionist and I was shocked to hear that the guy I had been talking to had actually left the Company! She didn't ask me why I was calling, but instead put me straight through to the Company's Legal Director. I later found out that there were some 'issues' over the Sales Director's resignation, and all his calls were being put through to legal automatically.

I told the Legal Director why I was calling; that I'd been waiting for an offer from the other guy, and could he tell me what was going on. To my surprise, he asked me to come in the same day to meet him, so I borrowed a car, threw on a suit, and shot down to their office in West London.

The story was remarkable. The week before, the entire Sales & Marketing team had up-sticks and left, to start their own competitive company, leaving just a few of the office staff, a couple of directors, and nobody else. The desks were piled high with lead forms and enquiry coupons, and the business was in a sate of panic because they had a massive advertising campaign running, but they weren't selling anything because they had nobody to process the leads and go out on the demonstrations and appointments.

I was hired on the spot. The next day I was given more ready-to-close business than I could ever have dreamed of, and awarded the outgoing Sales Director's high-end BMW coupe as my company car. My previously indifferent sales career took off like rocket and I made more money in the next twelve months than I had ever imagined possible. Not only that, but it was the first step on the ladder to a ten-year career in the mobile communications industry that took me around the world, and I ended up as a Director and shareholder in an overseas cellphone company which sold out to, you guessed it, Vodafone!

The lesson is clear; if nothing happens within a few days of your application, pick up the phone. There could be any number of reasons why you haven't heard back, so be pro-active. That single call I made changed my life forever.

Four years ago, I was hired to turn around a French Company in the TV industry. Straight away, I needed to hire a number of people to bolster the marketing team, so I posted the jobs on LinkedIn, and my inbox flooded with applications. There was one particular role, the Marketing Communications Manager, which required someone based at our Head Office in Paris, but with first class spoken and written English, because the business was international.

I filtered the applicants and produced a short-list of five, who I called in for interview. Of the five, I liked two in particular, so I called them back for second interview, and chose one who had the right experience, the right location, was apparently happy with the remuneration package, but needed a month to resign from her existing job before she could join our company. I made her the offer, closed the file and got on with other things, instructing my PA to follow up and set up the new employee's office, PC, Blackberry, and all the other things we'd need in order to get her up and running in her important role as soon as she arrived.

After three weeks I was concerned that I hadn't heard from her, and she hadn't returned her contract of employment, so I had my PA call her up. We were surprised to find that her current employer had made her a better offer to stay, which she had decided to do. She claimed that she had sent me an e-mail the previous week to explain this, but I definitely had not received it.

Frustrated, and desperate, I went to plan B, which was to call up the second short-listed candidate, and offer her the job. Unfortunately she had already found another position the week before and told me that she was no longer available. It was one of those head-in-hands moments. It had been ten weeks since I'd placed the original ad on LinkedIn, none of the other candidates had been suitable, mainly because of location or language skills, and here I was, back to square one, with a mountain of work piling up and nobody to take it on. It's not the kind of role that I could fill with a temp, and I had nobody else in the organization with the necessary skills.

Sometime that day, my phone rang. It was always tricky for me if the office phone rang, because our receptionist didn't speak English but assumed that I spoke French, which I really didn't very well. The upshot of this was that I generally ended up saying yes to every call she tried to put through. On this occasion, was I glad I did!

On the other end of the phone was a guy called Jeff Degan, definitely not a French name, who told me he was calling to follow up on his application for the Marcomms Manager job. I quickly loaded up the original applicant list on my PC screen and found his name, and a note that I had rejected him on the first pass although he had good qualifications and experience, but lived in Rennes, a few hundred miles away. Since the company was not prepared to pay relocation costs, and we needed somebody fast, I'd simply discounted him. For some reason he hadn't received the rejection e-mail (that's French admin staff for you, I guess) so he was calling to ask what happened.

As it turned out, he was American, with fluent French language, married to a French woman, and currently couch-surfing in Paris whilst he looked for a new job, so that he could then move his family to wherever he ended up working. I asked him to pop round the next morning for coffee, and after an hour I hired him on the spot. He turned out to be a fantastic manager and fitted in straight away, and I had the pleasure to work closely with him for the rest of my time in Paris.

Once again, the same lesson, which should be clear to you now. Don't sit around waiting for someone to call you back; hustle. You have no idea of the strange and unpredictable things that go on at the other end of this thin communications channel you are part of. Those are two perfect examples of how a simple phone call can change everything.

The objective up to this point has been to do what you need to do to get an interview, or at least the chance to 'sell yourself' on the telephone to your prospective employer. Now its time to take a look at what happens next, specifically the interview process, and how to prepare yourself for stellar performance.

Interview Technique

So, you've scored an interview. It might initially be a telephone interview or video Skype, especially if you're a long way from the Company's offices. Whatever the case, this is a binary situation. You'll either pass or fail. So there's no second chance, and preparation is the discipline you need to focus on.

Perfect Telephone Interviews

Guess what. Everybody hates these. A telephone interview puts you under immense pressure because it's a very narrow communications channel, so you don't get to use your instincts, particularly eye contact and body language. But if that's the way the process is going for you, there's no way of avoiding it, so suck it up and get yourself ready.

First off, if there's even the remotest chance that the Company might call you out of the blue, you need to be ready to deal with that surprise phone call. Inexperienced recruiters or low-level staff in a selection and recruitment agency might do this. They have a list of candidates and they simply sit down at the start of the day and plough through them. I've also come across managers who (perversely in my opinion) use this tactic to catch candidates unawares and see how they respond.

So if it's going to happen, there's not much you can do about it, but there are ways for you to take control of the process, so you're never caught out unprepared.

First off, you need to be ready to handle such an interview, constantly, whilst you're on your job-seeking mission. Later in this section, we're going to look at the kinds of awkward questions you might be asked, and how to rehearse the answers you'll give. Ninety percent of candidates I've interviewed over my career simply weren't prepared for the difficult questions, and to be fair I rarely use the classics, such as "tell me something that you're not very good at."

But HR professionals, especially those new to the role, often employ these kinds of questions because they got them from a manual or a textbook. It doesn't matter, they are in control of the situation, so they can pretty much ask what they like. It's often not the actual answer you give, but the fact that you don't flap or panic, that will get your through these kinds of bizarre interrogations.

But maintaining a state of readiness 24/7 is hard. When you actually get on the phone with your prospective new boss, you can't be on the back foot. You probably can't be on the front-foot either, but if you're balanced, and you've had a few minutes to get yourself up to speed and into the zone, you'll be calmer, and that will come across clearly on the phone. The idea is that you come out of it as 'easy to talk to' which requires you to give the impression of confidence and competence, even if your little webbed feet are paddling like crazy under the surface.

My primary recommendation is to screen your calls. First; Make sure that the telephone number you have given in your application has Caller Identification (CLI), ideally your cellphone, and never pick up the phone to anyone whose number or ID you don't recognize.

Secondly: Set up your voice mail professionally, with a business-like, properly recorded welcome message. Make sure you record it in a quiet place, where there's no background noise, and don't be tempted to use music in the background.

Clear your throat, make sure your voice is working properly, smile whilst speaking (its remarkably easy to tell someone's mood from their voicemail welcome message) and keep it short. When you record, wait two or three seconds before you start, because sometimes the connection takes a moment to stabilize, especially mobile-to-mobile. The perfect script is:

"Hello. You've reached Rick Smith. I'm sorry I can't take your call at the moment, but if you'd like to leave your name and number, I'll call you back as soon as I can."

That's it. Play it back and re-record as many times as it takes to get it perfect.

When a call comes through from a number you don't recognize, let your voicemail take care of it, then check it afterwards. This buys you time to prepare for the actual call itself. Take as much time as you need to get yourself relaxed and calm, and in the right frame of mind for the conversation. Always anticipate that it's going to be a full interview, so make sure you're in a quiet place, with your Application Documents open in front of you.

One advantage of the telephone interview is that you can

anticipate the key questions, and have your answers written or printed out, so you won't get caught out unexpectedly. Just make sure you don't start rustling papers or typing on a noisy keyboard when you have the conversation. Ideally, use a hands-free device so you have both hands available, for taking notes and accessing your documents as you talk. If it's Skype, install Call Recorder and start it as soon as you're connected. A recording will be useful later when you review the questions and answers, and it also helps to hear it back in order to refine the way you deal with the next one.

Regarding accents; attitudes vary from country to country, and even city to city. You may think that it doesn't matter, but when the only channel is voice, it matters very much. You need to practice speaking clearly if you're going to be having telephone interviews, and although you may not be able or willing to change your accent very much, you need to be sure that the other person clearly gets what you're saying, and doesn't judge you because of the way you speak.

Practice the answers to some of the questions, repeatedly, and even record yourself saying them so you know that you're getting your message across. If you've written them out you'll need to make sure that the language sounds spontaneous, not overly rehearsed. Spend the time you need to do this; it's part of your mission, and a critical factor in whether you pass or fail the telephone interview.

As with all interview technique, don't waffle. As a rule of thumb, no answer should ever be longer than two minutes, even if it's complex. Ideally, you should aim to answer a question in thirty seconds or less, or you risk boring the interviewer and they will switch off, and mark you down mentally.

The trickiest question is the open-ended one, such as "Tell me a little about yourself". You need to have your elevator pitch ready for this, so you don't drift off into unnecessary areas. Tell them only what you want them to know about you in order to pass you in the process. Set up your three key highlights, which might be the same ones as you used in the introduction to your Résumé, and rehearse saying it until you have it firmly in your mind, so that when you have to do it for real you'll be confident that the answer you give is concise and informative. If you don't tell them everything they need to know, they'll ask you another question, so make sure you have back-up answers. We'll cover the tricky questions later in this section.

Don't be afraid of silence. If you've answered a question, shut up. Watch how interviews work on TV news shows (but not politicians, they want to keep talking until the lights go out). The perfect interview is one in which both parties speak for around the same length of time. In fact, if you can get the interviewer to speak more than you, psychologists have shown that you are more likely to leave a favorable impression. But once you've answered the question or made a point, don't be afraid to stop and let the interviewer make the next move.

At the end of the interview, your interrogator might say something like; "That's all I have to ask. Do you have anything you want to ask *me?*" This is very common and you need to have a few sensible questions prepared. If you only prepare one, it might have actually cropped up in the body of the interview, so you'll be left high and dry. If you feel that absolutely everything has been covered adequately, you might say; "No, I think you've explained everything perfectly, Thank You"

If you can't think of anything else to ask, there's a stock question you can fall back on which will not only do that job, but also move you a little bit further towards closing the 'deal' as it were:

"Can you please tell me what the next stage in the process will be?"

If you feel that you've had a particularly good interview, and you established some rapport with your interviewer, you can be a bit bolder, and say; "Can you tell me what happens next please?"

This will play well for you as an enthusiastic candidate. It also forces the interviewer to indicate (in many cases) whether they are likely to be taking you to the next stage. It's important to get as much clarity as possible throughout the whole process, because you don't want to spend time waiting around for a call that never comes, or a rejection that will upset you when it drops on your mat or into your inbox. You're on a mission, and dead time when you're not out there hustling is a complete waste. As pilots say "there's nothing so useless as runway behind you!"

You can also ask how long it will be before they'll be advising candidates about the outcome of the interviews. You need to know this, because you're working to a plan, and once again you don't want an open-ended timetable that puts you on hold when you could be getting on with another opportunity.

Never be afraid to ask how you got on. The best way to frame it is this; "Can I ask if you think you'll be taking me through to the next stage?"

The worst that can happen is that they say No. At least then you'll know for sure and you can move on. If they do say no, which is rare, you'll have the chance to ask if they can give you any advice on why your application or interview wasn't up to scratch, so you can improve your presentation the next time. People are often disarmed by directness from candidate, but it doesn't mean they'll judge you negatively. And you might learn something important that will help you the next time.

Just be sure, when you ask any of these closing questions, that you don't come across as pushy, cheeky, or impertinent.

Always say *Thank You* before you hang up the phone, and mean it. And never ever follow up yourself with an e-mail to thank them for the interview, or add any supplementary questions. It's creepy. I once interviewed an excellent candidate who sent me a thankyou letter the next day, complete with claim for his traveling expenses, which had never been mentioned or offered. Had he not, he would definitely have been short-listed for the next stage. As it was, he was off my list straight away.

However, if a few days go by, and they've gone past the deadline that they told you at the interview, you need to pick up the phone and ask if anything's happening. If it's Human Resources, they'll be expecting these calls if they're running behind schedule. If it's the manager himself, you might get through to his assistant, who should be able to give you the answer. There's usually a perfectly reasonable explanation and you need to know it, because you're on a mission. Just be very polite and direct, without sounding impatient. If they're considering you, they'll want to keep you warm in case you're chasing any other opportunities.

Perfect Video Interviews

More and more companies are using video Skype for interviews these days, so you need to ensure you are set up and prepared for this. Once again, you should never accept an unsolicited video Skype call without having the opportunity to prepare. If you ever do answer a Skype call, you'll know who is calling, because it's impossible to call someone on Skype unless you've previously exchanged contact information, so at least you'll be forewarned. Never ever accept a video Skype or Facetime interview call on a smart phone. It looks and sounds unprofessional, and it's hard to control the environment, which as you know is something you should always try to do.

Virtually all laptops, and many desktop computers, including all modern iMacs, have webcams built in. They also have internal microphones, but these are not always that good, so you need to test your technical set-up before you embark on video interviews. Here are the rules:

1. If you answer a call in relation to your job search, never answer with the video switched on. Always answer it audio-only, and then you can take a moment to compose yourself and check that your environment is correct before you switch on the video. If there's a problem with the way you look or the situation you're in, make the excuse that your bandwidth is a little unreliable, and offer to call back in a few minutes.

2. Test your set-up. Skype with a friend, and preferably one who lives some distance away so you know that the line quality is going to hold up OK. You need them to tell you how the audio sounds and also if you are

sufficiently well lit.

3. If your inbuilt microphone isn't doing the job well, use a headset. Ideally use the ear-bud type that comes with your smartphone, because a big pair of studio headphones will not give the right impression. Even if your inbuilt PC microphone works fine, if there's background noise in your environment, use a headset anyway. Be careful of feedback, which can occur if the microphone and speakers are too close together.

4. Obviously if you're going to be using Video Skype, you'll need to be dressed and groomed appropriately. Unlike a real-life interview, nobody will be expecting you to be dressed in a suit and tie, or whatever is appropriate for the ladies, but you do need to be tidy and smart, and shaved (men, mainly) with your hair brushed. I know that beards are in fashion at the moment, especially what we used to call 'designer stubble' but you must understand that beards of any kind can be yet another polarizing factor in people's first impression of you. Nobody ever gets judged for being clean-shaven. My personal opinion, as a serial interviewer, is that ladies should be made up as if for work (not for clubbing), long hair should ideally be tied up or back, and definitely no cleavage on show. That may work for some, but it's considered unprofessional by seasoned recruiters. You don't want your appearance to be the reason why people remember you. Stand out but blend in. Remember, you may be at home, but that's not the appearance you are trying to give, and that goes for both men and women.

5. Take care of the background and anything that is going to be in shot when you're on screen. If you're room is cluttered or full of junk, move everything out of shot. You should be aiming to have a plain or neutral background behind you, so the focus is on you, not your environment, Once again, people make snap judgments when they see you for the first time, and your Bob Marley Rastafarian Bong on the bookshelf is not going to play well at corporate HQ.

6. Make sure you are lit from above or in front, never from the rear. If there's a window behind you, you'll need to draw the shades or close the blinds. If you don't you may appear as a dark silhouette on their screen, and that's not a good look.

7. Camera positioning and technique is very important. You need to position your camera, ideally at the top of your screen, so that when you are looking at the screen it appears that you are looking at the camera. There's nothing more irritating than someone who has their camera offset to the side, so when you are speaking to them they look like they're staring at something other than you. If your camera is at the top of your screen, move the video window as near to the top as possible, and shrink it as small as you can reasonably see. That way it will look like you are making eye contact, which is important in all interview situations.

8. It seem obvious, but if there are other people in the house, or if you are Skyping from your office, lock the door, or at least let people know that you're doing something which requires you to remain undisturbed.

Nobody wants to see your five-year-old's teddy bear or hear your wife telling you to take out the trash half way through one of the most important conversations of your life.

9. Turn off your cellphone. That means off, not vibrate or silent alert. And close all the other programs on your PC screen with the possible exception of documents you may need to refer to during the interview. It's especially important to shut your e-mail client (e.g. Outlook) and any other messaging applications, not just to minimize them, because if alerts come through they will be heard at the other end of the line. You need to focus, and any distraction will be considered rude by the interviewer.

If you are a regular Skype user, most of these tips will be obvious to you. Many of them are simply good manners. Remember, if you are one of a number of people being interviewed this way, the better the experience for the interviewer, the more favorably you will rate on their unofficial scorecard. You don't have to be perfect, you just have to be better than everyone else, and a few small details like this can make or break you.

The Q&A techniques for video interviews are half way between telephone interview and the real thing. On the upside, you can use notes and reminders to give you the answers to the tricky questions. On the downside you cannot be overtly seen to be referring to them, so you need to arrange things so you can unobtrusively read what you need, without shifting your gaze too far or for too long.

I have, several times, hired people on the basis of just a video interview, without actually meeting them face to face, and I know other people who have been hired this way. This is particularly possible if you are applying for a field-operative or international role, where the expense and logistics of bringing candidates hundreds or thousands of miles is simply impractical. It doesn't happen often, but it does nevertheless happen, so treat a video interview seriously, and give it at least the same attention to detail as you would a conventional interview.

Real Live Interviews

So, we've covered many of the techniques for interviews in the previous sections, and they carry through to the real thing. Of course, in a real interview, face to face with your interviewer (or interviewers, because there may be more than one) you won't have the luxury of being able to refer to notes or pre-prepared questions and answers, but nevertheless the same questions will come up, so you'll need to rehearse them in advance.

Don't wait until you have an interview confirmed to start preparing for these. The questions are pretty standard, and they'll come up time after time. Who knows how many times you may have to go through the process? But you will definitely have to do it at least once if you're serious about your job search, so it's all part of your general planning and preparation process.

Perfect Interview Preparation

But before you get to the interview itself, here are some important points to take on board;

1. Find out who will be interviewing you. If it's the HR department, they will usually be running a cull to produce a shortlist to put forward to the Departmental Manager or Director who will be making the eventual decision. If you get a letter or an e-mail inviting you for interview, it will normally say who you are meeting. If it doesn't, contact the sender and ask. It's important,

because unless you know, you can't prepare properly. Check them out on LinkedIn, and see what you can learn about them. You should be able to ascertain their age, their job function and seniority, and where they have worked before. You are looking for several things

a. Do they have anything in common with you? Did you attend the same school, do you support the same sports team, are you a similar age, ethnicity, or anything else that might enable to you to generate some empathy when you meet?

b. How long have they been in their role or company? If they've been there a few years, depending on the size of the firm, they will be more likely to be assessing you in terms not only of your suitability for the role, but also in terms of your fit with the Company's culture, so that will point you at another area of research where you can get ahead of the competition. If they haven't been there long, it's likely to be a more 'tick box' interview at the first stage.

c. What is their history? Have they come up an academic route (such as an MBA) or do they look like they're time-served. The former is likely to put more emphasis on qualifications, the latter on relevant experience.

Learn everything you can about who you will be meeting. Knowledge is power. You won't exactly know how to use the information you have until you're sitting across the desk, but at least you'll have something extra in your war chest that will put you ahead of most of the other candidates. But on no account ever give away the fact that you've been researching them personally. That's borderline stalker behavior.

2. Research the Company. One of the most common interview questions is "What do you know about our Company?" You should have a short, no more than two minute, answer prepared. Don't blow smoke up their ass; they won't like it if you're fawning or sycophantic. Just find out some salient facts about their products, their markets, their key customers, and so on. Most Company Websites have a 'Press' or 'News' section where you can easily find out what they've been doing, and what they're proud of in recent months. Try to stay current; nobody is impressed by old news. Don't be objective; don't express your own opinions on whether things are good or bad; simply pick one or two nuggets out of what you find and build a little statement around them. A typical answer to this question might be: *"Well I know you've been in business for over fifty years, and you sell your Widgets all over the world to some big companies. I even own a car that has some of your triple-flange devices in the suspension! I also saw that you made some interesting acquisitions recently, which is one of the reasons why I was motivated to apply for a position here."* That's plenty. It shows you've done your homework. You'll need to have more up your sleeve, but keep your powder dry, and only prepare as much as you'll need to answer the question honestly and concisely. Don't get involved in discussions about profit and loss, or the stock price. That's impertinent, and probably (technically) way above your pay grade.

3. Plan your day. Don't leave anything until the last minute. If you've never been there before, use Google Maps and even Google Earth to check out the location, so you'll know what to look for when you arrive. If you're having a morning interview and your journey is long, consider checking in to a hotel nearby the night before. You won't look or feel great if you had to get up at four in the morning and travel six hours. Make sure you know how long it's going to take to get there. It's a cardinal sin to arrive late for an interview, and even in the best-case scenario you'll be panicking and you'll get off on the wrong foot. Make sure you have the contact phone number in your cell, in case something unforeseen happens on the way.

4. Don't get drunk the night before. This is so obvious, but the temptation if you're sitting alone in a hotel room in a strange city may overcome you. I've not only interviewed candidates who were clearly the worse for wear, but I've actually done it myself, in Taiwan. Luckily I'd already secured the job and this was a final chat with the CEO before I signed my contract, but I felt dreadful, I must have looked dreadful and I definitely wasn't thinking clearly.

5. Learn to manage your nerves. The most important thing is that you allow plenty of time for everything leading up to the interview. Everyone gets nervous, even us old hands, and the stakes may be high for you, so you're bound to have a few butterflies beforehand. But don't add to them by getting yourself into a panic situation. Interviewers know that people get nervous, so they make allowances for a certain amount, but you can't

afford to fluff your lines, so you need to take the calmest possible approach to this in the days and hours leading up to the interview. The two most important things you are aiming to radiate are Confidence and Competence. It's the simple things, like not drinking too much coffee, and a few long, deep breaths before you enter the building that will help you keep a lid on your nerves.

6. If you smoke, definitely don't have a cigarette once you've showered and dressed for the event. It's a complete falsehood that nicotine calms the nerves; it's a stimulant and it will only make you worse. Plus, non-smokers can smell you a mile off, and it's a big turn-off for most people these days. You can smoke a whole pack afterwards, if that's what floats your boat. But on the day of the interview, don't smoke beforehand. If an interviewer ever asks you if you smoke, lie. Say no. That is all.

7. Don't get there too early. You ideally want to arrive at reception around fifteen minutes before your appointment. That gives you time to adjust to the surroundings and calm yourself down, but its not so long sitting in reception that you'll look like a lost dog. For men, if they ask you to sit down, try to remain standing, but unobtrusive. If you're wearing a suit, sitting will crease your jacket and may bag your trouser knees. You want to look good when you first meet your interviewer, because their first impression of you will be almost entirely based on how you look, and will set the tone for the interview.

8. If you are wearing a tie, make sure it is knotted neatly

and pulled up tight, with your shirt button closed. If it's a more casual environment and a necktie is inappropriate, never have more than the top button undone on your shirt. You are not Simon Cowell on X-Factor. Even casual business attire has standards and protocols. In terms of your general appearance, you should look as good as you can. No short cuts.

9. If you have tattoos, hide them. If you have piercings, beyond normal earring piercings for women, take them out. If you wear a lot of jewelry, particularly rings or bracelets, take them off before you leave for the meeting. A wedding band or a signet ring is fine, but a fistful of half-sovereigns is inappropriate. Remember, you will always need to adapt to the cultural norms of any company, and you may be able to relax back into some of your personal habits later on, once you have your feet under the table and you've worked out the lay of the land. But for an interview, you need to sanitize your image so that there is no possible chance of polarization, bias, or prejudice. And if in doubt, get a haircut.

10. When someone comes out to fetch you, always assume it is the person who makes the decisions. It doesn't matter if it's only the office junior; her impression of you may be included in the decision process, so put on your best face, smile, and be polite. Always offer a handshake; never go for a hug of any kind (too familiar) even if you know the person socially. This is a place of business, and unless it's France or Italy, man-hugs are probably viewed as strange or creepy.

11. Always have a cloth handkerchief in your pocket and be

ready to whip it out and wipe any perspiration from your face and hands. You may have walked in from a Great Lakes blizzard into a super-heated office building, and you may be dripping with sweat, but you need to take every possible step to look cool, calm and collected. If you have arrived with a few minutes to spare, ask the receptionist if you can use the rest room; check yourself in the mirror and wash your hands. Make sure you dry them properly; nobody responds well to a clammy handshake.

12. When you are being taken through to the interview room itself, whoever is leading you, don't initiate small talk, If you're asked about your journey, or the classic "So you had no trouble finding us?" keep your answers short and respectful. Nobody will care that your flight was delayed by fog, or the taxi driver nearly ran over a dog. Chattering is a symptom of nerves, and it's irritating. You need to keep your mouth firmly connected to your brain, and don't let the voices in!

13. When you're introduced to your interviewer, be ready with a firm (not hard) handshake, but don't offer it unless it's offered to you. In all senses, you need to adapt to the social and professional level of the person you're meeting, so be a follower, not a leader. Don't speak unless you are spoken to, and never interrupt or talk over another person. Keep some kind of smile on your face, but try to be natural throughout.

14. If they offer you coffee, the polite answer is "If you're having one". You might be better advised to ask for plain water, simply to lubricate your mouth one you

start speaking. But be aware that any liquid in the vicinity of a nervous person has a high propensity for spillage. I've seen it numerous times and it's always embarrassing, for everyone in the room.

15. Your interviewer will normally have your résumé and application letter in front of them, so you'd better know it off by heart, especially your dates. They may ask you to tell them something about yourself. Stick to the script. Make sure what you say is concise and positive, and corresponds with what you have written. Don't waffle, they'll ask you questions if they want to know more about anything.

16. Don't ramble. You've rehearsed the answers to the major questions you'll be expecting, so keep them short and relevant. Never disrespect a previous employer or colleague, no matter how hard you're provoked. The dignified professional way to behave is to keep things to yourself, and simply make light of any provocative challenges. They might say something like: "I've heard ABC Widgets is a difficult place to work?" Your answer should be something like: "No more or less than anywhere else, I guess!" If you're asked if you know somebody, simply answer yes or no. Don't offer any sentiments or opinions on the person concerned, and if you don't know them, say so. You may be having your honesty and integrity tested. Don't ever pretend; you will be caught out in the end.

17. Maintain eye contact as much as possible. Don't stare around the room, and try not to look away if they ask you a difficult question. Human beings instinctively

'calibrate' each other when they meet, and if you have to dig deep for an answer to a question, you may naturally look away, and it might be misinterpreted as lying. So practice strong eye contact in the days leading up to your interview. It's difficult, but do your best.

18. Never swear or curse, even if you're telling a funny story, and even if the interviewer swears like a navvy. It's not cool. Don't get drawn into discussions about religion, politics, sport, immigration, sexual proclivity, celebrities, or any other potentially divisive subjects, even if there's evidence of the interviewer's interest in the subject. That's not the kind of empathy you're looking for, and it's too risky. Some interviewers may try to take you there. If you feel like this is happening, your most dignified escape route is to say something like, "that doesn't really interest me" or "that's not something I really like to talk about." Just leave it there.

19. Don't be flustered or chaotic. If you have things in a bag or briefcase, make sure you can get at them easily if you're asked. Turn your cellphone off the minute you arrive in the building, and don't turn it on again until you leave. Never, ever open your laptop on someone else's desk. I've seen it happen, and it's just plain rude.

20. When the interview is over, don't be in too much of a hurry to stand up and leave. You need to make a dignified exit, because in the same way that your first impression will dictate the tone of the meeting, your last impression will leave a memory with your interviewer. Once it's over, make sure you've covered everything and asked the closing questions about what happens in the

next steps. Smile, stand up, carefully arrange yourself, shake hands, and leave with a smile on your face.

21. Never forget why you're there, and always expect the unexpected. No matter how well prepared you are, there will always be something that happens that you haven't planned for, so you need to be alert to your surroundings and take a breath if you're faced with something unusual.

Perfect Interview Answers

There's no need to go into how you answer questions about your experience or qualifications, because you should have been rehearsing those right from the start. The simple formula is:

- Know yourself and your subject.
- Keep your answers brief.
- You may add, but never deviate from what is written in your résumé, and what they can find out about you online, for example from your LinkedIn profile.
- Stay positive about your experiences and achievements. Everything you have done was a stepping-stone to where you are now, so be proud, but not conceited.
- Stay as far away from personal matters as possible. You're not a clone, but your private life is simply that, and nobody's really interested.
- If there's something about you that you worry might come up and be an issue, make sure you have a smart, explanatory answer ready.
- Never volunteer information that isn't asked for or required.

- Don't bullshit if you don't know the answer to something. Just say "I don't know" and move on.
- Don't talk about hobbies and interests voluntarily. If you're asked, pick just one, and make sure its something that could never be suspected of impacting on your work life. The best fallback is "I enjoy spending time with my family at the weekend."
- Never indicate that you have any money worries or domestic problems, even if you have.

The Difficult Questions

Everybody's worst interview fear is being asked a difficult question that they can't easily answer. But these questions are pretty standard so I've been constantly amazed over the years that candidates aren't better prepared. These are easy to rehearse, and to have the answers ready to trot out if the interviewer decides to go there. Remember, especially if an HR professional is interviewing you, these questions are not designed to get information, but simply to assess how you perform under pressure. Here we go…

Tell Me About Yourself

This is usually one of the opening questions. Don't be tempted to give a commentary on your complete résumé. Don't mention personal information when you answer. There are four topics; childhood, education, work history, and recent career experience, which is the most important. You answer could be:

"I was brought up in England, where my parents ran a small business. I went to school in London until I was twelve, and then we returned to the States and settled in Chicago, where I finished

school. I got my degree in mechanical engineering at MIT, where I also met my fiancé, who is now my wife. After college, I went to work for Boeing in Seattle for five years, in the design office. After that I was head of widgets at Bombardier in Quebec, which is where I've been for eight years now. We'd like to move somewhere closer to my wife's family, so when I heard about your recruitment drive for Engineering Managers, I decided it was time to take my next big career step.

So if I were to ask (someone you didn't particularly get on with), what would he/she say about you?

Spin this from a negative to a positive, like this;

He would probably say that I was impatient! But the truth is that I'm quite demanding on my team and myself, especially when it comes to deadlines. Someone who might not share my sense of priorities could misinterpret that.

What's the biggest risk you've ever taken?

Avoid describing a risk that you took with your Company's assets, and make it personal about yourself:

"I guess leaving a secure position at Boeing and moving all the way to Canada might be viewed as risky, but I was driven to take a step up in my career, and I knew I'd have to step outside my comfort zone sooner or later. I was sure it would work out, and of course it did."

Have any of your bosses ever challenged your decision?

You need to be ready to show humility and your ability to accept direction from above and the lesson you gained from it. Try:

"Once or twice. Each time, I've listened to their arguments and we've work out a way of achieving the objective based on their

strategic big picture and my tactical energy. I've learned along the way that the boss is usually right, and it's his neck on the line if I misjudge the situation or get it wrong."

Are you here to take over my job?

"Only if you move up and carry me with you! Loyalty is very important to me in business, and I've observed that you generally get back what you give."

What happens if you don't get promoted in a few years. How will you feel about that, because it's not guaranteed?

"I'm realistic about that situation. I can only do my best for the company, and grow in my role. If that gets me advancement in the future, that's great. But ambitious as I am, professional fulfillment also means a lot to me, and that can come in many different forms."

What is your biggest weakness?

This is almost always a trick question. You might want to answer: *"I don't have one"* but that's too trite (even if you don't) Try this:

"I can sometimes get a bit frustrated with people who don't demonstrate the same commitment as me, but I know that everyone's pressures and challenges are different, so I've learned to keep it under wraps and try to motivate and coach them to a higher performance level"

You've changed careers in the past. Are you sure this isn't just another expensive experiment that we'll end up paying for?

"I firmly believe that I'm a better, more grounded employee because I've learned some diverse skills in those different cultures and environments. My first career wasn't what I thought it would

be, but I was quite young and it took me some time to find my groove."

Your last Company failed spectacularly.   If you knew things were bad, why didn't you jump sooner?

"I was so focused on working to hold on to my job that I just didn't have time to look for another one. With hindsight I could have reacted sooner, but I put my trust in the management, and unfortunately they couldn't keep us alive. But I tried to do my part and gave it my best shot!"

I see you've been fired in the past. How did you feel about that?

"It was a shock at first, but I thought about it afterwards and determined never to let it happen to me again, which has made me much stronger. I managed to bounce back and get a new job with more responsibility, more money, and at better company, so on the whole it was a positive experience."

If you were in charge here and the market was declining for a particular product, what would you do?

"I would mobilize the commercial team to actively search for new markets for that product or a derivative, and encourage engineering and marketing to collaborates on upgrading or re-tasking the existing product to address the new requirements of the original market."

At your age, why you would be ready to take an entry-level position here?

"Occasionally you might need to take a step back to move your career forward. I'm ready and willing to learn your industry from the ground up, using my previous experience and maturity to accelerate the process."

We are an equality-based employer company, but our customers are Arabian and we were planning to hire a man for this particular job.

"Really? I have the ideal qualifications to do this job as well, if not better, than anyone else, male or female. I've done a lot of work in the Middle East and I've never found my gender to be an issue in the past."

Why did you take such a long career break, and why do you want to come back to work?

"When I had my children, my husband was working so hard to build up his career, so one of us needed to be full time raising the kids. I loved being a full time Mom, but I never lost my passion for work. I stayed in touch, doing some freelance work, and now the children are at school and we can afford day care if they're not, it's my time to re-start my career."

What would you do if you found the perfect female candidate for your team, but your boss insisted on hiring a man?

"I'd try to persuade him to hire both for a trial period. Whatever my preference, he might be right, so comparing them side by side would probably be the fairest way."

How many hours a week do you usually work?

"It's never been a set pattern for me. I'm comfortable with long hours during the week, if that means I can relax and do my own thing on the weekends. I've never let going-home time interfere with hitting deadlines, and I'm awake early anyway, so there are always a few extra hours every day to stay ahead of the curve."

Do you prefer "managing up" or "managing down"?

"In my previous roles I've always tried to find the balance of both,

and I don't see it as an 'either/or' situation."

Ask for permission, or beg for forgiveness?

"It depends on my boss. Some empower you, and you carry the can if it crashes, and they don't really want you asking for permission for everything. Others want to be involved in every decision, and generally they'll have a lot to add or teach. It depends on the skills of the people concerned, so it's horses for courses, I guess."

How have you handled company politics in the past?

"I've had line managers try to get me to collude with them against my better judgment. I've always tried to find a smart way through, which protected the company's best interests first and also kept the peace. The worst thing I've found is to stoke the political fire, so I let my work do my talking for me."

Has one of your bad decisions ever cost your company money?

"No. Absolutely not."

Lucky or Skillful? Which is best?

"I don't think it really matters how lucky you are; if you aren't applying the right skills, you won't last long!"

Where do you see the peak of your career?

"Every day is a new peak for me, as long as I keep growing and developing. Right now I can't envision a time when that will change, but ask me again in twenty years and my answer might be different!"

Have you ever found it acceptable to break confidence?

"Yes, when someone was open with me about something dangerous and unethical. I had no choice but to ensure it was dealt with before the consequences became irreversible."

Do you see yourself as leader?

"I do. I've observed the core qualities of leaders and I identify with many of them, in my small way. I get what people need from their leaders, and I work hard to listen and learn, then apply myself to providing that direction. I always keep one eye on the big picture, so I can guide my teams towards the key objectives. I can be tough, but only if there's no other way."

Describe your dream job?

"This one! That's why I applied!"

Finally

That's it. If you've read all the way through and you apply the recommendations and systems, you'll be armed with most of what you need to nail the job you want.

Each of the sections in this book is intended to tune your performance by a few percent in the right direction, which will give you a definite competitive edge over most of the other candidates in any hiring situation.

Just to be clear, I don't sell recruitment consultancy or anything like that; I'm much too busy with my own commercial and writing projects. However, if there's something in this book that isn't clear to you, or if there's a particular tactic that really works, I'd love to hear from you. Please e-mail me on **ricksmith@marketaccess.tv**

Likewise, if you should spot any typo's (sometimes they slip through the edit) I'd also love to hear from you by e-mail.

Finally, if you enjoyed the book, or even if you didn't, I'd really appreciate an honest review on Amazon. If you're reading the Kindle version, the next page will pop up and you can do it in about thirty seconds. I'd really appreciate it.

Of course, all of this advice and experience counts for nothing if you don't add the final important ingredient: **You!** Be yourself, and immerse yourself in the process. There are millions of unadvertised job vacancies out there. The Western economy is bouncing back with a vengeance, and there's never been a better time to be on the move.

Good Hunting!

You can check out all my books on the Amazon Store, available in Kindle and Paperback editions.

  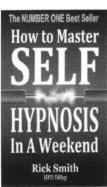

Just type *ricksmithbooks* into Amazon's Search

Printed in Great Britain
by Amazon